G000126262

EXTREME CUISINE

Eddie Lin

Exotic tastes from around the world

FROM THE AUTHOR

The only difference between 'tasty' food and 'nasty' food is one letter. I don't say this just to be flippant, or cute – it's just that, in much the same way, it can be a small twist that causes a food to be perceived as good or bad, and that twist is often in who is doing the eating. Food is a very cultural, very personal experience. Indeed, it's as much about the mind as it is about the mouth. When it comes to food that is unfamiliar, the mind determines exactly where this food rests within one's culinary comfort zone. A slice of processed American cheese hermetically sealed in plastic may speak of the wonder years to one person. To a Sardinian gourmet, *casu marzu*, a sheep-milk cheese infested with cheese-fly larvae, is the height of home and hearth and the absolute definition of comfort food. On the flip side, both of these cheeses can be thought of as food nightmares – it just depends on who's doing the eating.

In order to write a book like this one, it was imperative that I be open to a variety of foods. Some people consider themselves gustatorily liberal, but when push comes to shove, or when eggs over easy become *balut*, these eaters curl up into a foetal position – much like the prehatched duck in the *balut*. As a guy who, like an undernourished zombie, was voraciously devouring pig brains at six years of age, to me it's not only a matter of powering through a menagerie of strange chow, thumping my chest triumphantly upon keeping the meal down and then writing about it. The challenge is also appreciating why a delicacy can be construed as revolting by someone less adventurous.

I think most of the delicacies in this book are scrumptious and it's my hope that readers might be swayed to add some of these experiences to their own must-eat menus. Take baby steps. Start with the lime green Jell-O salad and move up to the blood tongue – they're sort of related in a gelatinous way. Trust me, they're both good. And, like my mother always told me: 'You'll never starve if you eat everything'.

Speaking of whom, I'd like to thank my mother for serving me that first dish of pig brains when all of my other friends were eating macaroni and cheese. Also thanks to my dad for allowing my mum to spend the grocery money on the weird stuff even though he hated it. Thanks to my wife, Diane, and girls, Chloe and Phoebe, for letting me subject them to all kinds of odd eats and for leaving me alone as I wrote this book. Thanks also to Eric Alba and my wife for guidance. Thank you too Janet Chute, Mark Moss and Scott Ahlberg for your exotic eats expertise. Finally, many thanks to Lonely Planet's Ellie Cobb, Jessica Crouch and Kate Morgan for their patience and kindness in shaping this book.

AUTHOR BIO

Since ingesting his first plate of weird food, Eddie Lin has wandered the earth seeking to sate his lust for the next strange bite, wherever it may lie. This former breakdancer turned food writer traded in his adidas for a fork and a laptop. Eddie's work has been printed in many publications including *The New York Times* and *The Guardian*. He has appeared on *Travel Channel*, *Playboy TV* and *CSI: NY*.

CONTENTS

SNAP IT UP, BEFORE IT SNAPS BACK AT YOU.

WHAT IT IS

Some foods mingle scrumptiously like star-crossed lovers. The bacon-wrapped hot dog comes to mind. Other foods just boggle the brain and make you wonder 'WTF?' Say hello to the alligator cheesecake.

WHERE IT IS

It's brought to you by New Orleans, the town that's turned tossing beads and flashing breasts into an art form. Jacques-Imo's Cafe, a Cajun-Creole restaurant and unofficial carnival under one roof, is where you can eat it.

HOW IT WORKS

Wild creatures revel in Louisiana's swamps like the other 'wildlife' does on Bourbon St. Alligators are abundant in the wild as well as on farms, so they're worked into the local fare whenever possible – in this case, a savoury cheesecake.

THE EXPERIENCE

This is cheesecake with a bite, and not just because of the gator sausage. Its spicy and sweet seasonings will make you take notice, much like you would if you were staring down the swamp beast. The fusion of meaty alligator sausage, snappy shrimp and creamy filling make the cheesecake's texture as exciting as the spices.

» Order it here, and don't forget your beads. Let the good times roll! ***Jacques-Imo's Cafe*** *www.jacquesimoscafe.com; 8324 Oak St, New Orleans, Louisiana, USA*

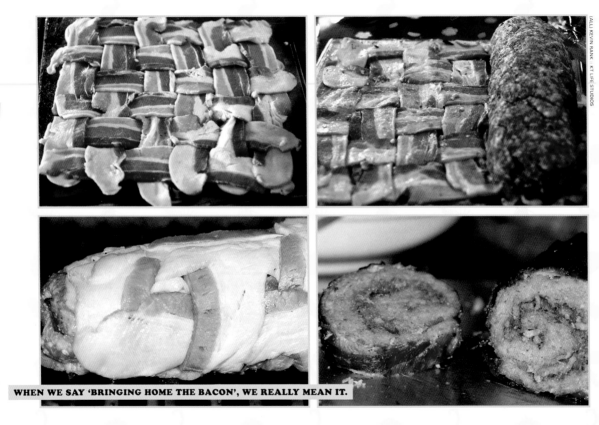

WHEN WE SAY 'BRINGING HOME THE BACON', WE REALLY MEAN IT.

BACON EXPLOSION: USA

WHAT IT IS

The internet is a marvel. One day something doesn't exist, and the next it explodes all over the world. The Bacon Explosion is one such eruptive thing. This extreme carnivore concoction is the invention of two Kansas City competition barbecuers who were challenged to create something incorporating bacon. A massive, smoked bacon-and-sausage log was the result.

WHERE IT IS

It's not available in stores…yet. However, you can easily make it yourself by following the recipe online.

HOW IT WORKS

Get 1kg of thick-cut bacon and 1kg of Italian sausage meat. Weave some of the bacon into a 12.5cm-by-12.5cm mat. Layer the sausage meat over the bacon mat. Chop and crisp up the remaining bacon, then distribute it evenly over the sausage layer. Season the meat and then roll up the bacon beast into a log. Smoke cook the log at 107°C for about 2½ hours. Sauce, slice and eat. Have a defibrillator standing by.

THE EXPERIENCE

This is a pork-on-pork orgy – it's fat with meat, tender and crispy, sweet, spicy, savoury and succulent. There is no more perfect an example of something so bad for you tasting so good. The danger here lies not with the bacon exploding, but your heart doing so.

» For step-by-step instructions, go to the Bacon Explosion's official website. **BBQ Addicts** *www.bbqaddicts.com*

TENDON EATERS: ALWAYS FENDING WITH BENDING.

BEEF TENDON: CHINA

WHAT IT IS

A connective tissue that, if masterfully cooked, will also connect your mouth to a unique and delicious food experience. There is nothing else like the texture of a beef tendon, which is like dense savoury gelatin. When prepared properly, it is as satisfying as any premium cut of beef flesh.

WHERE IT IS

Authentic Chinese restaurants all over the world have this collagen-saturated bit of cow on the menu, and it's on heavy rotation at dim-sum (yum cha) parlours everywhere. Just flag down the dim-sum cart and request a tin before they're all snapped up by hungry diners. Great Taiwanese beef-noodle houses know how to transform this challenging body part into a perfect complement for their steaming bowls of chewy egg noodles.

HOW IT WORKS

Not quite meat and not quite bone; the only way to cook tendon is by simmering or braising it at low heat for a few hours. This style of cooking also allows the soy sauce, rice wine, anise, rock sugar and other seasonings to penetrate the dense tendon.

THE EXPERIENCE

The mucilaginous texture of beef tendon may repulse some, but it attracts others. Toothsome, slimy, substantial and drenched with beefy, sweet and savoury flavours, tendon is intoxicating for those who can connect with it.

>> Send in the tendon. *Yong-Kang Beef Noodle Restaurant* +886 2 2351-1051; No 17, Lane 31, Sec 2, Jinshan S Rd, Da'an District, Taipei City, Taiwan

A TASTE FOR BLOOD DOESN'T MAKE YOU A VAMPIRE, BUT AVOID GARLIC AND CRUCIFIXES JUST IN CASE.

BLOOD: GERMANY

WHAT IT IS

Blood is the essence of life, yet most people don't consume it as a distinct form of nutrition. That could be the result of the stigma attached to vampirism, or that the major religions forbid its ingestion. The sight of blood can be unappetising to some. But blood as a food is nutritious, versatile and even tasty.

WHERE IT IS

Most people who have blood lust prefer it from a pig or cow. One very interesting plate of plasma is presented as a German cold cut called *blut zungenwurst* (blood-tongue sausage). It's made with cow blood and tongue, turned into a loaf, then sliced for sandwich meat. Another bloody treat comes in cubes. Pig blood is congealed and cooked and the result is 'blood cake', as it's known in China. Blood cake can be dipped into a chilli-soy sauce or placed into a stew of pork offal.

HOW IT WORKS

Congelation or solidification are the keys to preparing blood for a meal. Otherwise you'd be drinking it. These characteristics make blood a versatile ingredient for many dishes.

THE EXPERIENCE

Ever cut your finger and then suck the blood? Did it taste salty and slightly metallic? Yeah, animal blood is pretty much the same.

» Blood tongue is not a death-metal band. It's a sausage that even your grandma would love. ***Liehs & Steigerwald Homemade German & Specialty Sausages*** *+1 315-474-2171; 1857 Grant Blvd, Syracuse, New York, USA*

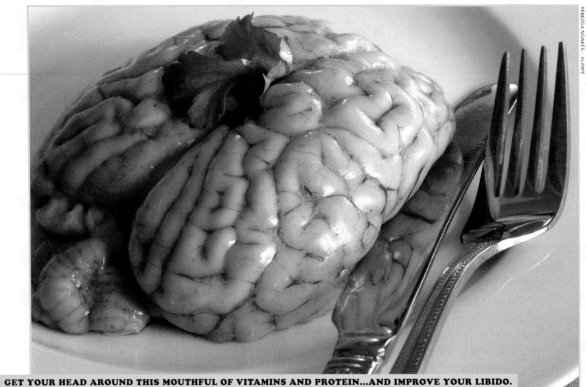

GET YOUR HEAD AROUND THIS MOUTHFUL OF VITAMINS AND PROTEIN...AND IMPROVE YOUR LIBIDO.

BRAIN: MEXICO

WHAT IT IS

It's not just a meal for zombies – all types of animal brain are consumed by humans as a delicacy. Sometimes revered as gourmet food, mostly rejected as taboo, brain – and the concept of eating it – can make you think quite a bit. Loaded with protein and vitamins, brain is pretty good for you, apart from all the cholesterol.

WHERE IT IS

At the height of the bovine spongiform encephalopathy (mad-cow disease) epidemic, cow brain was impossible to obtain, as the disease was fatal to humans who ate the brain of the infected cattle. Mexican restaurants used to be a reliable venue to score *sesos* (beef brain) tacos. Now restaurants are slowly reintroducing cow brains to diners.

HOW IT WORKS

Once cooked, brain can be eaten straight out of the head, as is done with fish brain in Asia and sheep brain in Norway. Brain can be battered and fried, or it can be scrambled with eggs. Pork brain is delicious steamed with ginger and soy sauce.

THE EXPERIENCE

For something that acts as the control centre of the body, the brain is a big softy. It has the consistency of dense tofu and the creaminess of a rich pâté. The savoury flavour of brain is very subtle. Some cultures believe that eating brain will make you better in bed rather than smarter in the head. Go figure.

» Don't think too hard, just eat it. ***Carnitas Michoacanas*** *+1 818-343-0203; 18507 Victory Blvd, Reseda, California, USA*

YOU'LL FIND NO PARTRIDGE HERE, BUT THEN THIS ISN'T YOUR AVERAGE PEAR TREE...

PRICKLY PEAR CACTUS: MEXICO

WHAT IT IS

Nopales are the young pads of the Indian fig opuntia variety of cactus, also called prickly pear. The *nopal* is common in Mexican cuisine and not considered strange by Mexicans, but for the newbie it's seen as an odd food.

WHERE IT IS

This needle-riddled cactus is found throughout the Americas and is almost as much of a staple ingredient in Mexican kitchens as the chilli. It's a major crop for Mexican farmers, who produce about US$150 million worth per year.

HOW IT WORKS

Once the prickly pear has been stripped of its prickly spines, what you do with it depends on your imagination. It can be consumed raw and sliced into a salad, grilled, boiled, fried with eggs, mixed into a taco or even infused into ice cream. Considered a healthy food, it's high in dietary fibre, loaded with several vitamins and minerals and is noted for treating diabetes. Strangely, for a plant that can hurt by touch, it's very helpful as a food.

THE EXPERIENCE

Its flavour is much more subtle than its menacing appearance: it has a touch of tartness with a crisp or slimy texture depending on how it's prepared. A *nopal* is a shadow of its former self by the time it's plated, and it just seems like any other vegetable. No pricks allowed.

» I hate to needle you but you should give these prickly pears a go. **La Cueva del Chango** *www.lacuevadelchango.com; Calle 38, Playa del Carmen, Quintana Roo, Mexico*

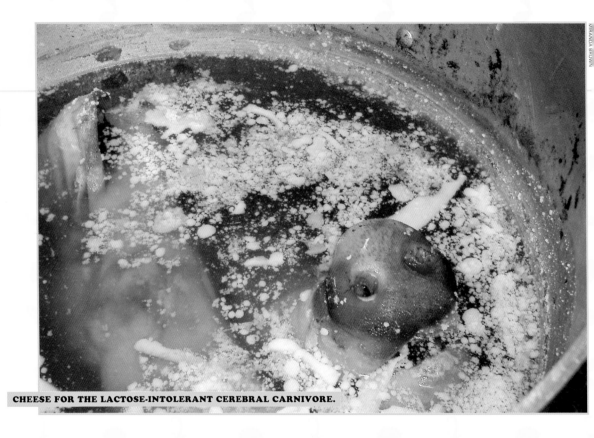

CHEESE FOR THE LACTOSE-INTOLERANT CEREBRAL CARNIVORE.

HEAD CHEESE: EUROPE

WHAT IT IS

Yes, it sounds like a problem that only a strong shampoo can cure. But head cheese is actually a cold cut that's fashioned from meaty bits taken from the head of a cow or pig.

WHERE IT IS

Head cheese can be found worldwide, although it goes by different names in different places. In Germany it's called *sülze*, in Denmark it's *sylte*, and in Italy it goes by *coppa di testa*. Most fine delicatessens sell this most heady of sandwich meats.

HOW IT WORKS

The animal's head is simmered until the flesh falls off the skull. The remaining meat is picked off the head, chopped and placed into a terrine. The cooking juices, which now contain the skull's collagen, are poured over the meat. Upon chilling, this collagen solution turns into a type of gelatin. After refrigeration, the head cheese solidifies into an aspic punctuated with meat chunks. Slice thinly for sandwiches.

THE EXPERIENCE

The flavours of the meat and the gelatin collaborate with a variety of seasonings and spices – including cloves, thyme, garlic and allspice – to create a satisfying carnivorous experience. Head cheese is luxuriously tender and moist, with a taste dynamism that will go to your head.

» Head to this restaurant to try it. **Babbo Ristorante e Enoteca** *www.babbonyc.com; 110 Waverly Pl, New York City, New York, USA*

'WAITER THERE'S A FLY IN MY CHEESE.' 'YES SIR, JUST WAIT UNTIL IT'S HAD BABIES.'

MAGGOT CHEESE: SARDINIA

WHAT IT IS

Here's where we separate the men from the boys, and the ladies from the girls. *Casu marzu* means 'rotten cheese' in the local dialect of Sardinia, Italy, but it goes much further than that. It is, more accurately, a maggot-infested cheese.

WHERE IT IS

First, know that *casu marzu* is illegal. Italians can be epicurean extremists, but even they draw the line somewhere. Maggot cheese is illegal for a very good reason – it can make you sick to your stomach, literally, with intestinal myiasis. If you don't chew the living larvae out of your maggot cheese, then expect these little nasties to hook into your intestinal lining and begin burrowing. It can result in abdominal pain, vomiting and diarrhoea. Rumour has it that if you look hard enough in Cagliari, you might just find some.

HOW IT WORKS

This mad cheese begins life as a completely sane chunk of *pecorino* that's then set outside to attract *Piophila casei*, also known as the 'cheese fly'. The fly, like a good mother, turns the cheese into a cozy nursery for her hundreds of squirming larvae.

THE EXPERIENCE

Mucilaginous and moving, *casu marzu* tastes of absolute rot and decomposition, with a lingering note of vomit. It burns.

» Poke around the Cagliari market, bond with the stall owners using your shoddy Italian, then casually ask if they have 'extra-special cheeses' not on display. **Mercato di San Benedetto** *Via San Francesco Cocco Ortu, Cagliari, Sardinia, Italy*

A HOT BEVERAGE YOU CAN REALLY GET YOUR MOUTH AROUND.

CHICHA: LATIN AMERICA

WHAT IT IS

Perhaps the easiest way to get this fermented drink is to be as rude as possible to your bartender and with any luck he'll supplement your beer with a wad of saliva. But that would be cheating. Traditionally, it's necessary to have corn, cassava or fruit masticated and moistened by Inca women. They spit the juice and saliva into a bowl, which is then allowed to ferment for a few days.

WHERE IT IS

The old Yiddish proverb 'Don't spit into a well, you might drink from it later' doesn't apply in chicha country. In the Amazon Basin there are many varieties. Go to Bolivia to experience maize chicha; rice is used in Venezuela. Chileans like their drink made with apples or grapes. The town of Otavalo in Ecuador celebrates chicha with a festival.

HOW IT WORKS

The key ingredient, whether it's corn, cassava or fruit, must have its starches broken down and converted to sugar. Some chicha utilise human spittle as a catalyst for breaking down the solids. Others boil the ingredients for this process and then ferment after cooling.

THE EXPERIENCE

Flavours vary due to such factors as whether the chicha has been fermented or is fresh, the type of plant or fruit used, flavourings and, not to mention, the source of the spit, but expect a sweet taste.

>> Head to Ecuador in the first week of September. *Yamor Festival* Otavalo, Ecuador

THE ULTIMATE KNEES-UP FOR CHICKEN LOVERS.

CHICKEN KNEE: CHINA

WHAT IT IS

File this under the category 'nothing goes to waste'. It takes a frugal cook to turn the dumpster-destined chicken knee into a culinary delight. This diminutive joint that's mostly cartilage can be transformed into an addictive treat. Eating more than a few may conjure up visions of dozens of sad, kneeless chickens.

WHERE IT IS

Some street-food stalls and dim-sum (yum cha) places serve these joints of chicken, especially in cities with large Chinese populations. New York's Yakitori Totto restuarant skewers and grills chicken knees to smoky perfection, Japanese yakitori-style.

HOW IT WORKS

As a dim-sum dish, the chicken knee is battered with a garlic-seasoned flour and deep fried. The result is a crunchy, chewy and slightly meaty bit of chicken that resembles a large piece of popcorn.

THE EXPERIENCE

A chicken knee is much easier to eat than the name suggests, since there is no bone. Cartilage, a small amount of meat, fat and skin may all be eaten. These elements join forces in creating the perfect snack of chicken with flavour and texture that is more complex than most small bites.

» Chinese. Japanese. Chicken knees. Try some. Yum! **Yakitori Totto** www.torysnyc.com; 251 West 55th Street, New York City, New York, USA

SOME YAKITORI DINERS GET A RAW DEAL...AND LOVE IT THAT WAY.

RAW CHICKEN: JAPAN

WHAT IT IS

Some of the early rules you learn about food include: don't eat things dropped on the ground, don't drink spoiled milk and never ever eat chicken that's not fully cooked. So eating *tori-sashi* (raw chicken) may be *the* biggest food felony, deserving of a death sentence. However uncommon, salmonella food poisoning may just be that death sentence. Still, that doesn't prevent some people from throwing caution to the wind, and raw chicken down their throats.

WHERE IT IS

Yakitori restaurants are Japanese establishments that specialise in grilling chicken and all its tasty parts from gizzard to gullet. Normally everything is grilled except for *tori-sashi*. Outside of Japan, say in the US, finding *tori-sashi* at a yakitori may depend on how diligent the local health inspectors are.

HOW IT WORKS

The logic goes that if the chicken is fresh and sourced from a clean farm, then the chicken is safe to eat raw or rare. Sometimes when ordering your *tori-sashi* you'll be given a verbal warning about the risk of salmonella when eating raw chicken. Once you've agreed, you're served the raw chicken accompanied by soy sauce and a heap of wasabi.

THE EXPERIENCE

Most people use the phrase 'tastes like chicken' when describing a new flavour. Ironically, raw chicken tastes more like fish – specifically albacore tuna dipped in sauce. Chicken of the sea, for sure.

>> When rare is simply way overcooked, try *tori-sashi*. **Torimatsu** *www.torimatsu.com; 1425 W Artesia Blvd, Gardena, California, USA*

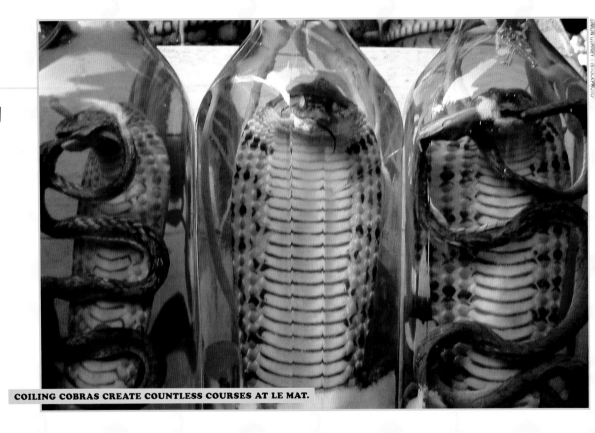

COILING COBRAS CREATE COUNTLESS COURSES AT LE MAT.

COBRA: VIETNAM

WHAT IT IS

Lately it seems like an entire television crew comes along with a multicourse order of cobra. Just about every travel or extreme-food show venturing into Vietnam has had a close encounter with a very angry cobra right before it's eaten on camera. Having video documentation of this extreme meal is probably more impressive than a 'Man Eating Cobra' T-shirt.

WHERE IT IS

About 10 minutes across the Red River from Hanoi is a village famous for its slithering-snake sampler platter. The place is officially named Le Mat, but everyone calls it 'snake village'. Le Mat is home to several restaurants that serve cobra.

HOW IT WORKS

Writhing snakes are presented on the floor only a few feet away from you. The grass snake pales in comparison to the cobra, which is larger with more meat, and 10 times the price of the grass snake. The cobra is killed when its head is slammed onto the concrete floor. The length of its underside is slit open and the beating heart plucked out. The blood and bile are collected in a cup.

THE EXPERIENCE

The cobra's still-beating heart is swallowed whole and chased with a snake-infused rice alcohol mixed with the cobra's blood and bile. Next, a variety of snake dishes are paraded out, from medicinal soups to crackling deep-fried snakeskin. Even the tiny bones are ground and fried.

» Get yourself along to the Le Mat Snake Festival, on the 23rd day of the third lunar month. *Le Mat, Gia Lam District, Hanoi, Vietnam*

COCK-A-DOODLE-DO! COCKSCOMB IS A MEAL TO CROW ABOUT.

COCKSCOMB: ITALY

WHAT IT IS

A rooster just wouldn't be a rooster without one, though hens have them also. The cockscomb is the floppy, red, royal crown atop a chicken's head. It's squishy and doesn't taste like much.

WHERE IT IS

Although not an easily sourced variety of meat, cockscomb theoretically is available wherever chickens scamper. There's an almost-forgotten Tuscan stew of chicken scraps that Italian peasants invented out of desperation. Chicken body parts like livers, hearts, testes and cockscomb were patiently cooked until they became edible. Some Tuscan restaurants still make the stew. Over in France, cockscomb is battered, fried and technically becomes fried chicken – chewy and crispy.

HOW IT WORKS

First, pluck any stray feathers from the cockscomb. Second, remove the outer membrane on the comb by blanching, then peeling. Once that's done, you can braise, fry, stew or do whatever you want to it.

THE EXPERIENCE

Ideally you should taste the essence of chicken, but cockscomb is most likely used in meals for mouth-feel purposes. Its subtle flavour is usually overwhelmed by its rubbery yet tender texture, and its alien appearance.

» How about trying some candied cockscomb for dessert? ***Incanto Italian Restaurant*** *www.incanto.biz; 1550 Church St, San Francisco, California, USA*

YOUR MUM MIGHT DISAPPROVE, BUT SMUT IS ACTUALLY TASTY AND HEALTHY.

CORN SMUT: MEXICO

WHAT IT IS

Huitlacoche is a Nahuatl term meaning 'raven's shit'. One look at it and you'll realise that the name contains little hyperbole. In the USA, farmers call it corn smut and want to smite the smut as quickly as possible. *Huitlacoche* is sometimes referred to as 'Mexican truffle', and apparently it can be delicious once you get used to it. Regardless of name, this is diseased corn where the kernels expand with tumours, which are then harvested and consumed.

WHERE IT IS

Only a warrior nation of Aztecs could be tough enough to deem *huitlacoche* food. This sort of corn cancer has parallels in flavour with the mushroom. Restaurants in Mexico regularly integrate this infection into a variety of dishes including crêpes, quesadillas and soups.

HOW IT WORKS

An ear of corn is infected by a plant fungus that causes the kernels to expand with tumours called galls. These galls are harvested while still immature (usually a couple of weeks post-infection) and moist; when mature they become dry and full of spores. *Huitlacoche* is seldom eaten plain, but rather as an ingredient within a dish.

THE EXPERIENCE

Corn smut is like a pulpy sludge concentrated with mushroom flavours rounded out by a slight corn sweetness and musty mould.

» Is it shit or truffle? That's up to you.
Los Xitomates *www.losxitomates.com;
Morelos 570, Col. Centro, Puerto Vallarta, Mexico*

TASTY TEATS ARE A TUSCAN TRADITION.

COW UDDER: ITALY

WHAT IT IS

What do you do with a cow's udder after it stops producing milk? Eat it, of course. However, it's not an easy cut of meat to track down, nor is it very popular. Maybe it's the idyllic image of the old-fashioned milk cow providing fresh milk for our morning cereal that's the turn-off. Maybe it's just too close to our own mothers.

WHERE IT IS

Using cow udder in cooking is a Tuscan tradition. It's the standard story of the poor using cast-off parts that the rich didn't want, then creating something edible that's sometimes delicious.

HOW IT WORKS

Cow udder is quite dense with meat, even if it doesn't appear so. The meat needs to be slowly cooked for it to turn out right, although there is also a Tuscan recipe for fried cow udder.

THE EXPERIENCE

It can be tender, like patiently cooked beef brisket. Strips of the meat are placed on toasted bread with a salsa-verde topping. It's just like beef, unless you happen to bite into a milk vein. Still, there's no milky flavour whatsoever. The lactose intolerant can be happy about that.

» Try it and become udderly surprised.
Nerbone di Greve www.nerbonedigreve.com; Piazza Matteotti 22, Greve in Chianti, Florence, Tuscany, Italy

FIVE LITTLE DUCKS WENT OUT ONE DAY, OVER THE HILLS AND DOWN THE HATCH...

WHAT IT IS

There is a special place for *balut* (egg with embryonic duck) in the annals of weird food. It is notorious in the same way that Genghis Khan was on the battlefield. For the uninitiated, fear and mystery surround this popular Filipino street snack. The *balut's* shell conceals a grotesque source of protein – an unborn duckling – adding flavour and distress to the meal.

WHERE IT IS

Pateros is a neighbourhood in Manila famous for its *balut* farms, but it's available from street vendors all over the Philippines, at all hours of the day. Just listen for the singsong *'balut'* call. It's like the Pied Piper of Pateros is calling you.

HOW IT WORKS

The duck eggs are gently incubated by replicating the dark, snug softness of a mother duck's bottom by using burlap sacks filled with rice husk. After 16 to 18 days, the *balut* is ready. Boil it for 30 minutes, then eat. Filipino men claim it's a powerful aphrodisiac.

THE EXPERIENCE

Firmly grasp the larger bottom part of the egg and tap the top portion to crack open a small opening. Toss in a pinch of salt and sip the soup (amniotic fluid). Then peel off the rest of the shell, season with salt, vinegar or chilli sauce, and eat. Since the duckling is not completely developed, it is very soft – including the bones and beak. The flavour is of egg, with a concentrated duck or duck-liver taste. Eat with eyes closed and hope there are no feathers to deal with.

» This Filipino seafood chain also carries *balut*. **Seafood City** *www.seafoodcity.com; 16130 Nordhoff St, North Hills, California, USA*

HARDER TO FIND AND MUCH TASTIER THAN THE WORLD WIDE WEB.

DUCK WEB: CANADA

WHAT IT IS

Duck web is not to be mistaken for duck feet, although that too is a delicacy. No, duck web – the webbing of a duck's foot – is special. It's entirely boneless, and that detail elevates duck web to gourmet status.

WHERE IT IS

Duck web and dim sum (also called yum cha) go together, since you can't make a meal of duck web alone. It's usually ordered from stainless-steel carts during dim-sum service, where many servings of various small bites are eaten throughout the meal. Fancier seafood banquet restaurants offering dim sum are more likely to have this eccentric item.

HOW IT WORKS

Boning a duck's webbed foot is a complicated matter. So complicated that, in fact, the procedure holds a US Patent. The maddening method involves multiple steps: freezing, thawing, slow cooking, cooling down, clipping toes, soaking in bleach and hot water, inserting a tube, yanking bones out by hand. And that's not all of it.

THE EXPERIENCE

Cooking duck web is infinitely simpler than boning the web. It's simmered, cooled and then tossed in spicy chilli oil. The crunchy, slick texture, reminiscent of kelp with dimples, is the main attraction. The spicy and delicate poultry flavour is secondary. No bones about it.

» Get caught in a web of duck. *Kirin Seafood Restaurant* *www.kirinrestaurants.com; 555 W 12th Ave, Vancouver, British Columbia, Canada*

OPEN YOUR LUNCHBOX, PINCH YOUR NOSTRILS AND TUCK INTO DURIAN.

DURIAN: ASIA

WHAT IT IS

The infamous durian fruit has been described in ways that would shatter anybody's self-esteem. The fruit emanates an odour that smacks of pig dung and all manner of rot, including corpses. With all that said, durian is still referred to by many loyal fans as the 'King of Fruit'.

WHERE IT IS

Where you won't find durian is on planes, trains, other public transport, many hotels and almost all restaurants. Even with these bans, people in countries like Malaysia, Singapore, Thailand, the Philippines and Taiwan delight in the durian's complex bouquet of foul and fruity.

HOW IT WORKS

When the King of Fruit is ripe, it falls from the tree and is caught by netting so as not to damage the fruit or crush the skull of a passer-by (a durian can weigh as much as 4kg). Brace yourself for a blast of fruit flatulence when you split it open. Use a spoon, not your fingers, to dig out the yellow, custard-like sludge – the stench will linger long after you've ingested it and your digits and friends will thank you for using cutlery.

THE EXPERIENCE

'Tastes like heaven, smells like hell.' It's generally agreed that the taste of durian is not nearly as intimidating as its funk. It's a mosh pit of flavours that include garlic, onions, caramel, stale cheese and strawberry, all eaten while in a porta-potty.

» Durian is far from mainstream in the USA, the UK or Australia, but in Singapore durian is fused into strudels, cakes, mousses, crêpes and cream puffs. ***Goodwood Park Hotel Deli*** *www.goodwoodparkhotel.com; 22 Scotts Rd, Singapore*

HERE'S THE GREEN EGG, BUT WHERE'S THE HAM?

1000-YEAR-OLD EGG: CHINA

WHAT IT IS

Call it '1000-year-old egg', 'century egg' or 'hundred-year egg' – whatever you choose, it's probably not the best name for a food. In fact, it's not even an accurate description – it requires much less time than 1000 or even 100 years to make. Try 100 days.

WHERE IT IS

Almost all Chinese grocery stores worldwide stock this East Asian staple. Many Chinese restaurants slice the dark-brown-and-green-hued preserved egg and add it to lean pork congee (rice porridge). Also, 1000-year-old egg is part of a variety of cold foods on a platter served at Chinese wedding banquets.

HOW IT WORKS

A duck egg is entombed in a paste mixture of tea, ash, lime, salt, clay and rice husk. Several eggs are then placed inside a cloth-covered container, where they remain for three months until the eggs' pH level has risen. The result is a dramatically altered albumen: it changes from white to dark amber. Likewise, the yellow yolk has transformed into a deep-green goop.

THE EXPERIENCE

'Ammoniacal' is not usually a word you want as a description for your food, but that's the first thing you'll notice when biting into the egg. The fetid flavour is quickly followed by a sulphuric one. The texture of the albumen is firmly gelatinous and the yolk is now a thick syrup. The experience is primordial, and the fact that this egg is named '1000-year-old egg' now doesn't seem like such an exaggeration.

» You've waited a long time for this egg, now eat it. **Congee Village** www.congeevillagerestaurants.com; 100 Allen St, New York City, New York, USA

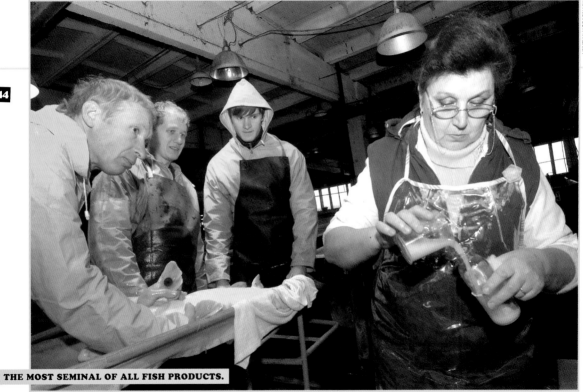

THE MOST SEMINAL OF ALL FISH PRODUCTS.

FISH SPERM: JAPAN

WHAT IT IS

Cod sperm or, politely, cod *shirako* is mostly eaten raw or slightly grilled, sometimes as tempura. The English enjoy their herring, mackerel or carp sperm (also known as milt) poached. However you down it, be prepared for a burst of flavour.

WHERE IT IS

As the old adage goes, there's plenty of fish sperm in the sea. Sort of. At least, it's plentiful in Japan. Many sushi restaurants serve sperm. *Izakayas* (Japanese pubs) may have a semen selection on the menu too. The season for fish sperm is generally in winter, before the spring mating season. Makes sense.

HOW IT WORKS

As with all sperm, *shirako* is delicate and can't be roughly handled or cooked. This is why the Europeans poach the milt and then make it even creamier with a cream sauce. The Japanese simply rinse the swollen, slick sacks of semen and put a handful into a dish of tangy ponzu sauce.

» Semen says, 'Eat this.' **Sushi Dai**
www.tsukiji-market.or.jp; Tsukiji Fish Market, 5-2 Tsukiji, Chuo-ku, Tokyo, Japan

WHAT'S GOOD FOR THE GOOSE IS GOOD FOR THE GANDER.

WHAT IT IS

Long before foie gras (fat liver) can be eaten, the source of the liver – a duck or goose – needs to eat a lot. In fact, the fowl must eat more than is natural, and foie-gras producers ensure this by force feeding it. The end result is a swollen liver six times its normal size.

WHERE IT IS

The Périgord region of France is where much of the world's foie gras is produced. The area is as saturated with foie-gras merchants as the poultry livers are with fat. Foie gras is obtainable all over the world, although it was briefly banned in Chicago and, in 2012, will be outlawed in California for animal-cruelty reasons.

HOW IT WORKS

A goose or duck is restrained while a tube is inserted down its oesophagus and a grain mash of corn is pumped directly into the bird's crop (where food is stored before digestion). Other methods of producing foie gras, claimed to be more humane, are being practised with mixed results.

THE EXPERIENCE

What all this force feeding has harvested is an unparallelled gastronomic experience that goes down much easier than a gavage feeding. Oleaginous, luxurious, creamy, light, meaty and buttery, a great piece of foie gras is just as much a memory wipe as it is delicious food. After the first intoxicating bite, you may wonder: what controversy?

» Fatten up with fat liver. *La Table d'Erillac* *+33 5 53-51-61-49; Place Eugene Le Roy, Hautefort, Dordogne, France*

REMEMBER THE STORY ABOUT THE FROG WHO WAS REALLY A PRINCE? TOO BAD, YOU JUST ATE HIM!

FROG: JAPAN

WHAT IT IS

When it comes to eating frogs, everyone, it seems, is a leg person. The rest of the frog seems to disappear. This is no surprise, really, since most of the meat is on the legs. The big exception is frog sashimi, where you'll eat everything but the ribbit.

WHERE IT IS

Frog sashimi isn't taking the world, or even Japan, by storm. Few sushi restaurants serve this multicourse meal of frog. One establishment is infamous for presenting its unique delicacy on television. The video is easy to find on the internet and gives a vicarious as well as extreme culinary experience.

HOW IT WORKS

Not only does this frog meal make use of the whole animal, it also requires that the frog is still alive while being eaten. This is a method of serving sashimi called *ikizukuri* (prepared alive). While alive, half the frog is skinned and its legs are removed, then the flesh is thinly sliced. The barely living frog is presented on the same platter as its sliced half. The frog gets to watch itself being devoured.

THE EXPERIENCE

Due to the fine muscle fibre of frogs, the meat is tender. Its flavour of fishy chicken is enhanced by a dipping sauce. And then unenhanced by the frog's ever-present gaze.

>> Frogs at this restaurant croak for your meal in more ways than one. **Asadachi Nishi-Shinjuku** *1-2-14 Shinjuku-ku, Tokyo, Japan*

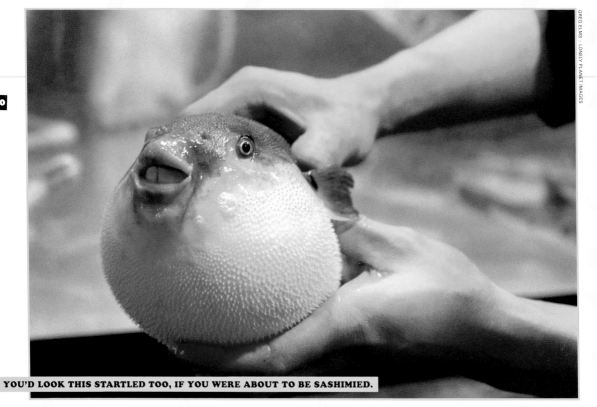

GREG ELMS :: LONELY PLANET IMAGES

YOU'D LOOK THIS STARTLED TOO, IF YOU WERE ABOUT TO BE SASHIMIED.

FUGU: JANPAN

WHAT IT IS

Tradition and honour dictate that if a fugu chef accidentally kills a customer by not preparing the fugu (poison blowfish) safely, the chef must commit *seppuku*, a Japanese ritualistic suicide by disembowelment. If that were truly the case and this tragic meal transpired, the body count would be at least three: the blowfish, the customer and the chef. It's the ultimate last supper, but at least the customer doesn't get stuck with the bill, which starts at US$250 per person for a multicourse meal that includes fugu prepared in several ways: sashimi, sake and stew.

WHERE IT IS

Puffer-fish-shaped lanterns signal a *fugu ryotei* (blowfish restaurant). The lanterns are harbingers of a risky meal, and can be seen ominously floating throughout Japan.

HOW IT WORKS

A pinhead's worth of the toxin in fugu can kill 30 people. The poisonous parts of the fish (especially the liver) need to be expertly removed by a licensed fugu chef before serving in order to avoid an causing excruciating death. Fugu flesh is sliced tissue thin, so thin that the ornate design on the platter shows through after the meat is plated.

THE EXPERIENCE

Nausea, dizziness, loss of motor skills: these are the dramatic symptoms of fugu poisoning. But your taste buds won't experience anything that dramatic. Fugu is virtually flavourless. Like serious poison should be.

>> Fugu. It's a meal to die for. ***Shunsagami***
+81 3 3343-4885; Odakyu Manhattan Hills 13F,
1-1-3 Nishi Shinjuku, Tokyo, Japan

EDDIE LIN

NOT GOOEY, NOT A DUCK; EAT IT RAW OR ADD A LENGTH TO YOUR HOT POT.

GEODUCK: ASIA/USA

WHAT IT IS

First off, it's pronounced *gooey duck*. Due to an apparent error in transcription from its original native American name, the word now baffles anyone attempting to pronounce it for the first time. Second, it's actually a clam. Finally, it's easy to spot geoduck at the market – it's the thing in the seafood section that looks like a gigantic penis.

WHERE IT IS

Geoduck is immensely popular in Asia, so much so that the status of this formerly cheap meat has been erected to luxury levels. To sample geoduck go to one of the many upmarket restaurants in Asia that serve the dish. But be prepared to pay – geoducks have been known to sell in Asia for up to US$60 per kg. If you'd rather eat one for free, start digging. They're most abundant in Puget Sound, Washington, USA.

HOW IT WORKS

In Korea, geoduck is marinated in a spicy chilli sauce and eaten raw; it also can be stir-fried or stewed. In China, it's widely thought of as an aphrodisiac and consumed hot-pot style. Americans in the northwest used to add geoducks to chowders. But the most common way to consume this phallic symbol of the sea is as raw sashimi.

THE EXPERIENCE

Looks can be deceiving. Although flaccid in appearance, the geoduck's texture is crunchy when raw, and firm when cooked. The flavour is sublimely sweet and slightly oceanic.

» Try some geoduck sashimi in Seattle. *Shiro's Sushi Restaurant* www.shiros.com; *2401 2nd Ave, Seattle, Washington, USA*

PUT A SPRING IN YOUR STEP WITH A HANDFUL OF GRASSHOPPERS, THE REBOUND ACE OF SNACKS.

GRASSHOPPER: MEXICO

WHAT IT IS

Instead of mindlessly reaching for the saucer of peanuts or bowl of popcorn while you enjoy that frosty cold beer at your favourite bar, consider snacking on *chapulines* (grasshoppers). They're high in protein like peanuts and crunchy like popcorn. You'll never miss the old snacks. Just mind the jumping legs getting stuck between your teeth.

WHERE IT IS

You'll find *chapulines* in Oaxaca, Mexico. It's where the Zapotec people have been munching on grasshoppers for thousands of years, and where you'll discover a world of insect exotica that most people will never know. At the Mercado Benito Juárez, peddlers hawk small and large *chapulines* from dizzying mounds. Oaxacan restaurants quickly put together tacos or guacamole with grasshopper as the main ingredient.

HOW IT WORKS

Young nymphs are favoured because of their tender texture and lack of wings. The *chapulines* are boiled, washed and then cooked – generally by dry frying them with a blend of lime, salt and chilli.

THE EXPERIENCE

Grasshoppers are crispy and of light flesh, and their natural grassy-earthy flavour coalesces with the sour, salty and spicy seasonings as nimbly as the bug takes to the air. However, they may carry roundworm parasites, and recently lead measurements in *chapulines* have been staggeringly high. So getting a leg stuck between your teeth may be the least worrying part of eating a *chapulín*.

>> Grasshopper, your first lesson: jump into my mouth. ***Mercado Benito Juárez*** *Oaxaca, Mexico*

A MOST VERSATILE PET: CUTE, EASY TO MAINTAIN, DELICIOUS.

GUINEA PIG: PERU

WHAT IT IS

They purr, chirp and whistle. They have big cartoonish eyes and look like toy animals. If you do a Google Image Search for *cuy* (their Spanish name), up pop pages of undeniably cute, adorable and huggable pictures of guinea pigs. Then there's that one image of a roast guinea pig on a spit, which somehow managed to slip through the SafeSearch feature. It seems they're not just cute, but delicious too.

WHERE IT IS

Most people can't handle dining on cute. Not so with Peruvians. They eat an estimated 65 million guinea pigs each year, so Peru is probably a good place to start. No Peruvian home is complete without a few dozen *cuyes* scampering about, nibbling on food scraps to fatten themselves up enough so that they can also become food.

HOW IT WORKS

First, just don't think about how darn lovable they are. Typically, *cuy* is either stewed or roasted. When it's stewed, *cuy* is unidentifiable and easy to eat. Roasted, however, it comes visually represented in full, from pointy nose to fat rear. It's not so cute anymore. In fact, it looks more like a rat. A delicious rat, no less.

THE EXPERIENCE

When roasted, a guinea pig looks like a rat and tastes like rabbit. The younger the *cuy*, the crispier the skin, and this is preferred. This cuddly fur ball will be but a memory with every succulent bite.

» Any restaurant on this plaza in Peru will serve you up some delicious *cuy*. **Plaza de Armas** *Cuzco, Peru*

AFTER A HEARTY MEAL OF HAGGIS YOU'LL FEEL LIKE BLOWING A BAGPIPE, TOO.

HAGGIS: SCOTLAND

WHAT IT IS

Haggis is the stuff of legend, and is viewed with great national pride – eating this offal dish is one way to ingratiate yourself with the people of Scotland. If you eat it while wearing a kilt, bonus points for you.

WHERE IT IS

Go to Scotland. The best places make this delicacy by hand using secret seasonings passed down through the generations. Most meat shops make haggis fresh on the premises. However, to truly pay homage to haggis, attend a Burns supper 'haggis fete', held on 25 January all over Scotland.

HOW IT WORKS

At a Burns supper, a man stands before the gathering, firmly wielding a large blade. On the table sits his target, a boiled sheep stomach encasing its own 'pluck': the sheep's heart, liver and lung, minced and mixed with oatmeal, suet, onions, stock and seasoning. The grand result is haggis. The man then recites 'Address to a Haggis', a poem by Scottish poet Robert Burns. As he bellows the words, 'An' cut you up wi' ready slight', the ceremonial dagger slashes open the taut haggis, liberating the steam and spilling forth the internal delights of the blackface sheep.

THE EXPERIENCE

Take a sip or three of whisky. Dish on some *tatties* (potatoes) and *neeps* (turnips). Be generous with the whisky sauce as it pours onto the haggis, unleashing the pâté-like flavours, onion bite and savoury seasonings of this 'Great chieftain o' the puddin'-race!'

» The haggis can be found at butchers across the UK. **JB Houston** www.jbhouston.co.uk; Greenbrae Loaning, Dumfries, Scotland, UK

THE MOST EXPLOSIVE AND (AHEM) FRAGRANT FISH YOU'LL EVER ENCOUNTER.

WHAT IT IS

First you need a can of the fermented herring called *surströmming*. This is easier said than done. Airlines have banned cans of *surströmming* from being brought aboard planes – thanks to the high-pressure fermentation of the fish, cans often explode.

WHERE IT IS

Head to Sweden. Very few restaurants offer *surströmming* on their menus because of the herring's overwhelming stench, but food shops freely stock it in cans. It's also available for purchase on the internet, where smell is less of a problem.

HOW IT WORKS

Baltic herring are caught in the spring during their spawning season. Unfortunately for the fish, however, they don't ever spawn – they end up fermenting for one to two months in a barrel. After the initial fermentation, the rotting process continues within the confines of a tin can, where the herring are portioned and packaged. Gases begin to build up, causing the can to bulge and round out like a tin ball on steroids.

THE EXPERIENCE

Be nice. Eat it outside. Its malodour can be described as a mushroom cloud of rotten egg and decayed fish in rusty solvent. Mercifully, the flavour is of salty and sour smoked fish, and not much more. Tone it down by eating it the traditional way on *tunnbröd* (a Swedish flatbread) with boiled potatoes, chopped raw onions and crème fraiche.

» Haven't you always wanted to taste something on an airport's security watch-list? ***Fiskevistet Mat o Café*** *www.fiskevistet.se; Skagsudde Skeppsmaln, Arnäsvall, Västernorrland, Sweden*

STRAIGHT FROM THE HORSE'S MOUTH...TO THE BUTCHER SHOP.

HORSE: JAPAN

WHAT IT IS

So hungry you could eat a horse? You better not be craving it in the USA. It's as taboo as wanting a cat burger or a dog sausage. The idea of eating horse meat is anathema to most Americans – in 2007 the last horse slaughterhouse in the USA was shut down. But the rest of the world doesn't seem to have as much of a problem consuming this high-quality equine meat.

WHERE IT IS

In Japan raw food isn't solely the realm of seafood. The preferred preparations for horse meat don't involve cooking: for example *sakura*, *basashi* and thinly sliced sashimi are all ways to serve horse. In Italy there's a horse stew called *pastissada*.

HOW IT WORKS

Horses are not raised for meat as other livestock such as cows and pigs are. When a horse ceases to be of use as a working or riding animal, it's sent to the 'glue factory', as the story used to go. In reality, most unproductive or even wild horses end up at a slaughterhouse, where a bulk of their parts will go towards pet food or human consumption.

THE EXPERIENCE

According to the United States Department of Agriculture, 'The meat is leaner, slightly sweeter in taste, with a flavour somewhat between that of beef and venison. Good horse meat is very tender, but it can also be slightly tougher than comparable cuts of beef. The meat is higher in protein and lower in fat.' Oh well, US consumer, you can always imagine.

» You can eat equine edibles, raw or cooked, in Canada. **Frite Alors!** *www.fritealors.com; 5235A Ave du Parc, Montréal, Québec, Canada*

IT SURE IS GREEN, BUT WE'RE NOT SURE WHAT THIS WILL DO FOR YOUR CARBON FOOTPRINT.

LIME GREEN JELL-O SALAD: USA

WHAT IT IS

This 'salad' is alien to some people, with its quivering, translucent green colour and strangely moulded gelatin that locks in anything from grated carrot to miniature marshmallows.

WHERE IT IS

Jell-O (jelly), the principal element of this deviating delight, is available in most countries, but lime green Jell-O salad can be traced to many American homes. To maximise search results, look to an area dubbed the 'Jell-O Belt', a region in the USA that includes Utah and portions of its neighbouring states, whose residents apparently really love Jell-O.

HOW IT WORKS

Lime Jell-O is dissolved in hot water and then placed in the refrigerator to partially set. Later, other ingredients such as juices, fruits, vegetables, cottage cheese and confectionery items are folded into the Jell-O. The whole shebang is then poured into a special mould and chilled in the fridge for several hours. The salad typically accompanies meat, acting somewhat like a dressing.

THE EXPERIENCE

Now that the salad (which usually resembles a spacecraft in which ET may have darted around the universe) is ready to eat, what's it like? It depends on the ingredients. It can be sweet, savoury or so spicy that your nose will run (because of the horseradish used in some recipes).

» The best way to sample this is to make it yourself, with one of many horribly unique recipes available online. **Simply Recipes** www.simplyrecipes.com

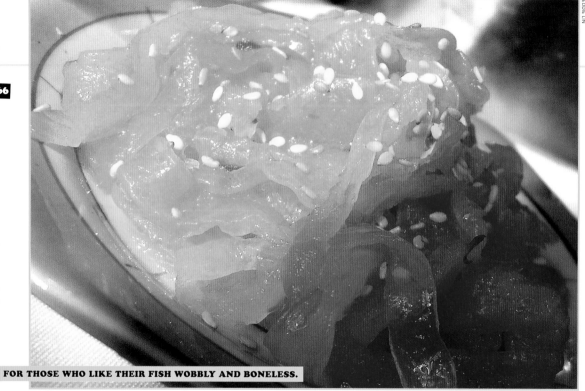

FOR THOSE WHO LIKE THEIR FISH WOBBLY AND BONELESS.

JELLYFISH: CHINA

WHAT IT IS

Jellyfish is the food solution in a world of environmental concerns such as overfishing, global warming and farm-irrigation runoff. Jellyfish thrive in these conditions, invading beaches and stinging sun-worshippers worldwide. It's time to get revenge. It's time to feast on jellyfish.

WHERE IT IS

The Chinese have been eating jellyfish for centuries. Many Chinese restaurants, from hole-in-the-wall places to grand seafood banquet halls, serve the spineless blobs. It's one of the most common items on the Chinese menu, yet many non-Chinese have never tried it.

HOW IT WORKS

Soak the jellyfish (a common variety served in restaurants is the cannonball jellyfish) in water, and refrigerate it overnight. The next day, drain and rinse well. Cut it into thin strips and quickly blanch in boiling water. Toss the cooked jellyfish in a dressing of soy sauce, sesame oil, rice vinegar and sugar.

THE EXPERIENCE

By the time the dish reaches the table, it doesn't resemble jellyfish anymore. It looks like strips of marinated daikon (Japanese radish). It's crunchy like daikon. However, it certainly is not a vegetable. Made up of 80% collagen, jellyfish is good for treating arthritis and bronchitis and lowering blood pressure.

>> Make a peanut-butter-and-jellyfish sandwich. It's easy. Just substitute your usual fruit jam with deliciously sweet and savoury jellyfish. Surprise your friends!

SURE TO PUT SOME BOUNCE INTO YOUR DIET.

KANGAROO: AUSTRALIA

WHAT IT IS

Although kangaroo has only recently gained momentum as an alternative meat around the world, Australia's indigenous people have been eating it for thousands of years, and have benefited from kangaroo meat's low fat and calorie levels and high protein. This bush tucker (native Australian food) happens to be quite delicious and is easy to work with in the kitchen.

WHERE IT IS

If you want to eat roo, you need to go to where they are. Australia is the only place kangaroos exist naturally in the wild; here, there are more kangaroos than humans. However, if Australian cattle and sheep farmers had their way, nobody would be eating this marsupial meat. Despite any opposition to eating kangaroo it's now widely available in many incarnations, from kangaroo jerky to roo stew.

HOW IT WORKS

Kangaroos are not farm raised; they're wild and free range. Commercial hunters are permitted to cull certain larger species to control the population. The roo's powerful hind legs are mainly used for human consumption. This versatile red meat is wonderful grilled, stir fried, cured, in a pie or in soup.

THE EXPERIENCE

Kangaroo tastes slightly gamy, but not in a bad way. It has the flavour of spirited beef without the negative components. When it's not overcooked, the meat is tender.

» Hop on the grilled kangaroo with tomato chutney. *Little Creatures Dining Hall* www.littlecreatures.com.au; *222 Brunswick St, Fitzroy, Victoria, Australia*

'HOW DO YOU TAKE YOUR COFFEE? CAPPUCCINO? DECAF?'

'NO, EXCRETED BY A CAT-SIZED MAMMAL, PLEASE.'

KOPI LUWAK: INDONESIA

WHAT IT IS

Kopi luwak: a coffee derived from beans consumed, digested and excreted by the common palm civet, a cat-sized mammal that sports the facial markings of a raccoon and is a relative of the mongoose.

WHERE IT IS

This dung delicacy hails from the islands of Sumatra, Java and Sulawesi in the Indonesian archipelago.

HOW IT WORKS

Palm civets dine on ripe coffee cherries located in Indonesia's treetops. The fruit is fully digested by the animal, while the bean remains intact. Farmers then pluck the beans from the faecal matter. After a thorough scrubbing, the beans are roasted, ground and brewed.

THE EXPERIENCE

The thought of drinking coffee once bonded by poop may make your stomach percolate, but don't knock it till you try it. The digestive process zaps the bitterness from the bean, creating a slightly sweet, rich flavour with less caffeine than your average cup of joe.

» *Kopi luwak* is one of the rarest beverages on earth. If you're not heading to Indonesia any time soon, high-end coffee shops will sporadically carry it. Prepare to shell out up to US$10 for a thimble-sized cup or over US$400 per pound. But beware of counterfeits. Make sure it passes the, um, sniff test.

LIP-SMACKINGLY GOOD AND LEERING AT YOU: LIVE LOBSTER.

WHAT IT IS

If you get an animated lobster, it will appear as though it's watching you eat it alive. A lively lobster adds to the restaurant experience, just like attentive service and a nice ambiance.

WHERE IT IS

Most Asian restaurants with a live-lobster tank will be able to whip up this delicacy, but it's not easy to order. Just as you always suspected, there are secret menus in Asian restaurants that are hidden in plain sight and written in the language of the cuisine's origin. Live lobster sashimi is sometimes on that menu, and sometimes it's not on any menu at all. You just have to know that it's available.

HOW IT WORKS

Once the lobster is cut in half between the abdomen and the cephalothorax, the chef must work quickly. The meat in the abdomen is separated from the shell and sliced into thin sashimi portions. The meat is then plated onto the empty shell. The cephalothorax is set on a bed of crushed ice. All of this is put together on a large platter. The task is performed so fast that the lobster's waning motor reflexes are still active.

THE EXPERIENCE

Cooked lobster is meaty and chewy, but live lobster is crunchy, moist and naturally sweet. Schadenfreude might be another flavour as you taste and watch the lobster's final moments.

» Eat some extremely fresh seafood. **Dynasty** *+86 21 6275-0000; Renaissance Yangtze Shanghai Hotel, 2099 Yan'an Xi Lu, Changning District, Shanghai, China*

EDDIE LIN

THE ULTIMATE VIKING SNACK: CAUSTIC, GELATINOUS SEAFOOD.

LUTEFISK: SCANDINAVIA

WHAT IT IS

This is stockfish, a dried white fish (usually cod) that has been reconstituted in a caustic lye-and-water solution then cooked, resulting in a gelatinous, jiggling slab of seafood with a foul stench all its own. Translated, *lutefisk* means 'lye fish'.

WHERE IT IS

Lutefisk is a food native to the Nordic countries, however, due to changing tastes, this fish dish is becoming less popular in its homeland but is gaining aficionados in the USA, particularly in the Midwest, where there are heavy concentrations of people of Scandinavian heritage. Most *lutefisk* is consumed during the winter holidays, when Lutheran churches commonly serve it at fundraising dinners.

HOW IT WORKS

Why the caustic lye? Legend has it that enemies of the Vikings poisoned their invaders' stockfish with lye. Eventually the Vikings ate the tainted fish and deemed it delicious, thereby reinforcing their tough reputation – as warriors and as diners.

THE EXPERIENCE

This is more chemistry experiment than fish fillet. In fact, if cooked too long, there's a risk of *lutefisk* saponifying into soapfish. There's a distinct chemical flavour to *lutefisk*, but when butter or rendered pork fat is added some say it becomes poor man's lobster.

>> Available year-round. ***Olsen Fish Company*** *www.olsenfish.com; 2115 N 2nd St, Minneapolis, Minnesota, USA*

SO WHAT IF IT LOOKS LIKE AXLE GREASE – IT'S GOOD FOR YOU!

MARMITE/VEGEMITE: UK/AUSTRALIA

WHAT IT IS

Ingesting Marmite or Vegemite is like eating the leftovers of someone else's meal, because this unique comestible is actually a yeast extract left over from beer brewing. People have strong opinions about the spreads and either love them or hate them upon first try. Regardless of flavour, it's generally agreed that Marmite and Vegemite are healthful foods.

WHERE IT IS

In Britain and New Zealand, it's known as Marmite. In Switzerland, they spread the Cenovis. Australians have a version of the yeast extract known as Vegemite. Both Marmite and Vegemite are owned by major corporations and can be found all over the world.

HOW IT WORKS

The basic method for eating this yeast extract is to lightly spread it on bread – a little goes a long way. But there are hundreds of ways to eat this stuff, including topping it on ice cream or, in Southeast Asia, adding it as a condiment to rice porridge.

THE EXPERIENCE

Marmite is sticky, supersalty and has the special savoury fifth flavour of *umami*, largely associated with meat or MSG. Vegemite is more like a beef bouillon. Marmite sold in New Zealand and Australia is sweetened a bit more than the UK version is.

» British celebrity chef Gary Rhodes has a Marmite menu from starters to dessert. ***Rhodes 24*** *www.rhodes24.co.uk; Tower 42, 25 Old Broad Street, London EC2N 1HQ, UK*

EDDIE LIN

IT'S HEALTHY AND RICH IN VITAMINS, SO KEEP EATING TO THE BITTER END.

WHAT IT IS

The Chinese have an expression for enduring difficult times that translates as 'eating bitterness'. It toughens you and builds character. The Chinese have a dish that can also be referred to as eating bitterness – the bitter melon. But bitter melon is a kind of bitterness that some people willingly eat and even enjoy.

WHERE IT IS

Resembling a cucumber with warts, the bitter melon is a fruit so bitter that Pulitzer Prize–winning food critic Jonathan Gold compares its flavour to cancer medicine. Cultivated in most of Asia, Africa and the Caribbean, the bitter melon is not too difficult to procure anywhere in the world. The Chinese use bitter melon in stir-fries and soups, and it's even dried and made into a tea called *gohyah*. *Karela gosht* is a Pakistani bitter-melon dish with lamb and spices.

HOW IT WORKS

To cut the bitterness, the fruit is sometimes sliced open and salted then washed. It can be blanched to further reduce acridity. Once prepped, the bitter melon is ready to cook.

THE EXPERIENCE

The flavour is acerbic, harsh, astringent and amaroidal. Did I mention bitter? Eating bitterness, however, does have a pay-off. Bitter melon is rich in vitamins and minerals, and has been shown to lower blood-sugar levels in diabetics. There is also early evidence that it can help fight HIV.

» Pakistani-style bitter melon and lamb: more bitter than unrequited love. **Dhanak Deira** *www.dhanakdeira.co.uk; 486 Blackburn Rd, Astley Bridge, Bolton BL1 8PE, UK*

A MEXICAN HANGOVER CURE – IT'S A LOAD OF TRIPE.

MENUDO: MEXICO

WHAT IT IS

Ideally you should have a hangover to nurse, though it's not necessary. *Menudo* is a Mexican stew made with large quantities of tripe (cow stomach). It's also heavily seasoned with chilli and oregano. These key elements combine forces and act as an elixir to soak up the excess booze and clear your head.

WHERE IT IS

Menudo is a former peasant dish that likely will never make the Taco Bell menu. However, it's widely available in many Mexican restaurants throughout the US and Mexico, as well as in parts of South America. It can be found in homes as well, if the cook is patient enough to make this time-consuming stew.

HOW IT WORKS

Honeycomb tripe and calf hooves are slowly simmered with *hominy* (a hull-less dried corn) and a host of seasoning and spices. It's then cooked for four hours and served with fresh tortillas.

THE EXPERIENCE

Not all *menudos* are created equal. Menudo is a bit like American chilli, with every recipe as unique as the individual making it. Well-crafted *menudo* renders the tripe delicate in flavour with little gaminess. The broth should be thickened a bit with the collagen from the calf hooves. There should be enough seasoning to take away the fog in your head, but not the taste of the ingredients.

▶▶ Don't just try it. Judge it. Pick the best *menudo* in Texas! ***Texas State Menudo Cook-Off*** *www.vivacincodemayo.org; Hays County Civic Center, 755 Civic Center Loop, San Marcos, Texas, USA*

THE BREAKFAST OF CHAMPIONS (WHO LIKE SLIMY, STICKY, STINKY FOOD).

NATTŌ: JAPAN

WHAT IT IS

Nattō has all the characteristics of things you should not put in your mouth. It's malodorous, slimy, sticky and foul flavoured. But this fermented soybean, which looks like it'll make you sick is actually good for you, with many health benefits. It's claimed that eating *nattō* can decrease your risk of developing blood clots and osteoporosis. Sometimes looks can be deceiving.

WHERE IT IS

Most *nattō* eaters elect to indulge their vice within the privacy of their own homes. *Nattō* is easily found in Japanese markets. The Kantō region of Japan seems to be where this gooey, rotten bean enjoys the most popularity.

HOW IT WORKS

Soybeans are steamed for six hours, then the bacterium *Bacillus subtilis natto* is introduced and mixed into the batch. The beans are then fermented for about 24 hours at 40°C. Finally, the *nattō* is cooled and aged for a week to develop its signature caramel consistency. Typically eaten for breakfast, *nattō* is best after being stirred, seasoned with mustard and soy sauce, and served on a bed of steamed rice.

THE EXPERIENCE

Even less attractive than *nattō* itself is having to watch someone eat it, so do it at home. Otherwise, you risk looking like a swamp thing with strings of *nattō* slime attached to your lips, stretching and contracting with each bite. *Nattō's* challenging texture is only matched by its musty, bitter flavour.

» Some Japanese restaurants specialise in this slimy bean. ***Tenmasa*** *+81 29-224-6460; 2-2-31 Miyamachi, Mito-shi, Ibaraki-ken, Japan*

KIND OF LIKE A SWAMP RAT, BUT BIGGER AND TURKEY FLAVOURED.

NUTRIA: USA

WHAT IT IS

Originally introduced to the United States and farmed or hunted for its fur rather than its flesh, the nutria (also known as the coypu) is a non-native rodent gone wild. With the demand for nutria fur all but vanished, many of these creatures have either been released or escaped into the wild, resulting in overpopulation and much negative environmental impact, such as vegetation destruction, river-bank erosion and the displacement of native wildlife.

WHERE IT IS

There was a time when the state of Louisiana and the US federal government invested millions of dollars in a war against the nutria. The Louisiana Culinary Institute even created a recipe for the meat – Louisiana nutria with mustard sauce (look it up on YouTube). Eateries in the region were encouraged to market the rodent as exotic and a delicious, healthy alternative to other meats. None of the culinary efforts saw success.

HOW IT WORKS

Since you can't buy nutria meat or order it in a restaurant, you'll have to get a hunting licence, grab a rifle and hit the swamp – shoot it, skin it and cook it.

THE EXPERIENCE

Nutria is a herbivore, which makes its flesh taste more like poultry – some say it's like dark turkey meat. So if you think you might enjoy the taste of an oversized rat with a hint of turkey flavour, gobble up a nutria.

» Nab a nutria and cook it with an official recipe from the Louisiana Department of Wildlife and Fisheries. ***Nutria.com*** *www.nutria.com/site14.php*

DRINK MODERATELY WHEN DOWNING THIS, OR YOU'LL END UP LEGLESS.

WHAT IT IS

To eat *sannakji* is to engage in a food fight with your own food. This may be the closest you'll come to experiencing what it might be like as a predator in the wild, taking down and eating your food alive. Except that this prey is accompanied with dipping sauces.

WHERE IT IS

This is Seoul food. The capital city of South Korea is brimming with eateries catering for every sort of appetite, including those craving undead tentacles. If you can speak Korean or you're with someone who can, you'll probably be able to score a plate of disembodied, animated baby-octopus tentacles at the local seafood restaurant.

HOW IT WORKS

The server will reach into a fish tank for a baby octopus not much bigger than a man's hand. The octopus' tentacles will then be quickly chopped off and further segmented into smaller pieces, which is crucial for avoiding asphyxiation by tentacle. All the writhing bits are speedily plated and presented with sauces.

THE EXPERIENCE

The taste is clean and oceanic, like an oyster's kiss. The texture is that of a viscous gummi worm. The attitude is vicious and vengeful. Even from beyond the grave, the octopus commands its angry appendages to choke the life out of you by any means necessary. Like your mother always said, chew your food properly.

» Eat with a good pair of chopsticks and a medical technician, in case an emergency tracheotomy is needed. ***Nak-ji-Chon*** *(Octopus Village), 105 Seoul San-ga shopping mall, Seoul, South Korea*

A TAIL OF FINE DINING, SLOW COOKED THE WORLD OVER.

OXTAIL: CUBA

WHAT IT IS

This former throwaway peasant piece of meat is made up of bone, fat, connective tissue and meat. It's usually slow cooked to take full flavour advantage of all these components. These days it's a premium-priced cut of beef.

WHERE IT IS

Anywhere there's a cow there's an oxtail dish. The Italians make a Roman stew out of it called *coda alla vaccinara*. The Cubans have a spicy oxtail stew called *rabo encendido* (tail on fire). The Chinese like to braise oxtail with star anise, Shaoxing wine and soy sauce. South Africans cook up a version called oxtail *potjie*, which calls for brandy and lemon.

HOW IT WORKS

Cook it low and slow, just as an oxtail moves in life. The low temperature and long cooking time help to break down the connective tissue and release the collagen, thereby thickening the stew and enriching the beefy flavour. Braising and stewing also keep the meat moist and tender.

THE EXPERIENCE

Oxtail is a rich and hearty meal. The flavours of the ingredients (including tomato, wine and garlic) fuse and are infused into the oxtail, making every bite burst in a savoury symphony. The moist and gelatinous texture forms a creaminess that no other cut of meat can easily achieve.

>> Heads or tails? Tails it is. Spicy Cuban oxtail, to be specific. ***Habana Mambo*** *www.habanamambo.com; 7420 Broadway Ave, North Bergen, New Jersey, USA*

IT'S NO COCK AND BULL STORY, PEOPLE REALLY DO EAT THIS.

PENIS: ASIA

WHAT IT IS

The hardest part about eating penis is not the actual eating but placing the order. If it's not uncontrollable giggling, beet red blushing or sudden loss of speaking abilities, it'll be something else that prevents you from asking for the bull penis on the menu. Which is perhaps why it goes by euphemisms like 'pizzle'.

WHERE IT IS

Pho ngau pin xe lua is Vietnamese *pho* (rice-noodle soup) with transparent slices of bull penis almost as thin as the noodles. In China, hot-pot restaurants offer plates of bull-penis shavings with Sichuan peppercorns, resulting in a penis that really burns. Cebu, a city in the Philippines, has roadside food shacks that have a mysterious item on their menus called 'soup number five'. Don't be fooled – it's penis soup, Filipino-style.

HOW IT WORKS

Bull penis is sliced finely because of its dense fibrous connective tissue. If not cut in thin wafers, then the penis needs to be simmered for several hours to break down the sinew.

THE EXPERIENCE

Yes, it's the ultimate aphrodisiac – Viagra before the invention of Viagra. Organotherapy is the concept of eating certain parts of an animal to help the eater's counterpart. Put simply: eating bull penis to help your penis. 'What you eat is what you treat' is how the Chinese saying goes. The difference is that this Viagra is a lot like beef tendon...rubbery.

» Don't be a dick. Eat one instead. ***Guolizhuang Restaurant*** *+86 10 6405-5966; 1A Dongyan, Xihai, Xicheng District, Beijing, China*

GUARANTEED TO BEAT THAT POSTDRINKING SINKING FEELING.

WHAT IT IS

What's tan and green and red all over? Nope, not a toad in a blender. It's a pie floater and it's a specialty dish down under. Exquisitely simple and infinitely satisfying, the pie floater is made up of an Australian meat pie that's placed upside down onto a heaping bowl of thick pea soup and topped with tomato sauce.

WHERE IT IS

Australia is the home of the pie floater, and Adelaide is ground zero. This hybrid meal of soup and pastry can be eaten in various incarnations around Australia, but the original version is offered by pie carts throughout Adelaide.

HOW IT WORKS

Get yourself a nice pastry stuffed with minced meat and filled with gravy, and gently plop it topsy-turvy onto a bowl of dense pea soup. Spatter on a layer of tomato sauce and eat while the whole shebang is still hot.

THE EXPERIENCE

Meat, vegies, grains – that's every food group in a single bowl. This is great weird food, and having a few drinks beforehand helps achieve maximum enjoyment.

>> Sydney isn't anywhere near Adelaide, but strangely it's the home of the most famous pie floaters in Australia. *Harry's Café de Wheels* *www.harryscafedewheels.com.au; Cnr Cowper Wharf Roadway & Brougham Rd, Woolloomooloo, Sydney, New South Wales, Australia*

FOR THE DINER WHO LIKES TO PLAY IT BY EAR.

PIG EAR: CHINA

WHAT IT IS

If you own a dog in the USA, you may have tossed it a dried pig ear to chew on now and again. For other cultures, though, pig ears are much too cherished and would never go to the dogs. They are a delicacy to be savoured in so many different ways.

WHERE IT IS

In China, cold pig ears that have been braised, stacked, chilled and sliced are popular snacks to pair with beer. Mexicans and people from the Japanese island of Okinawa share a love of pickled pig ears. Famous English chef Fergus Henderson puts a British twist on the Chinese version by using European seasonings.

HOW IT WORKS

Pig ear is stubborn as an ingredient because it's mostly cartilage. The most effective method to render it usable in the kitchen is to break down the collagen and cartilage by cooking the ear at a low temperature for a long time. The cartilage yields a bit but never softens.

THE EXPERIENCE

To the surprise of many first-time pig-ear eaters, the texture is crunchy. But for pig-ear lovers, the dense cartilage is part of its appeal. The gelatinous collagen, skin and fat do a brilliant job of holding in seasonings. Warning: by the time you finish a serving, you'll have developed a serious ear affection.

>> Nibble on some ear, darlings. *New China Club* www.newchinaclub.co.uk; 37 Chalton Street, London NW1 1JD, UK

THIS LITTLE PIGGIE WENT TO MARKET, AND *THIS* LITTLE PIGGIE CRIED 'WEE WEE WEE'.

PIG FACE: CHINA/USA

WHAT IT IS

People seldom appreciate where their food comes from, but if you happen to be eating a pig's face then this won't be a problem. Staring back at you is a tasty reminder of the provider. Until you scoop out the eyeballs, that is. Then it can't stare back at you, can it?

WHERE IT IS

Hole-in-the-wall Chinese barbecue restaurants display their wares of pork and duck in the window, hanging from hooks without disguise, without apology. This is what you'll be eating. You may as well introduce yourself. From Beijing to Brooklyn, these bold meat cases defy you to not look at your food source. If you're lucky, there may be an extra side of pig face lying on the bottom for you.

HOW IT WORKS

Nothing goes to waste in a Chinese restaurant. By the same token, not everything goes on the menu either, so if you want pig face you'll have to ask. Don't be embarrassed, there's no saving face when you want to eat pig face.

THE EXPERIENCE

Snap off the ear and eat it like a thick, crispy, chewy, greasy potato chip. Offer the eyeball to your elder or your lover, it's the proper thing to do. Be cheeky and eat the most tender bit of cheek. Flip the face, look for the brain scraps and eat your way to a higher IQ.

>> Face-off with pig face. **Sam Woo Bar B Que** *+1 818-988-6813; 6450 Sepulveda Blvd, Van Nuys, California, USA*

IT MAY LOOK AND FEEL LIKE OLD BIKE TYRES BUT IT'S SOUL FOOD.

PIG INTESTINES: USA

WHAT IT IS

Pig intestines are enjoyed all over the world, but when they're cooked up as soul food they become chitlins (short for 'chitterlings'). Usually chitlins are dished up as a stew, or battered and fried.

WHERE IT IS

You'll find chitlins anywhere there's an African American community that appreciates the tradition of American soul food.

HOW IT WORKS

A dish created from necessity and of slavery heritage, chitlins require much time and effort to cook properly. Pig intestines are filthy things that must be cleaned, washed, disinfected, boiled, washed and cleaned again. They're also scraped of all impurities, undigested food, faecal matter and even polyps. Only then are they safe to cook.

THE EXPERIENCE

In addition to the seasonings included in the dish, the taste of the chitlins will also be determined by the cleanliness of the intestines. A fetid flavour is guaranteed if the intestines weren't cleaned well. Otherwise, chitlins are somewhat bland in taste and diners usually douse them with vinegar and chilli sauce. Chewing on chitlins is a great exercise for the jaw – they can be chewy and rubbery. But that's part of their appeal.

» Join the chitlin circuit! *E.J.'s Soul Food Restaurant* +1 412-731-3000; 810 Penn Ave, Wilkinsburg, Pennsylvania, USA

EDDIE LIN

WHEN YOU SAID 'LET'S CHEW THE FAT' I THOUGHT WE WERE JUST GOING TO TALK.

PURE PORK FAT: UKRAINE

WHAT IT IS

Fat is the Paul Giamatti of foods. It's underappreciated, it's usually in a supporting role and, well, it's fat. It normally enhances the performance of other foods or aids in their cooking but rarely does it alone command centre stage. Not so with *lardo* or *salo*. These are unrendered fats that diners in the know celebrate.

WHERE IT IS

The Italians love their *lardo*, but if there are a people who love their pure fat more than the Italians, it has to be the Ukrainians – and that's saying a lot. *Salo* is practically the official food of the Ukraine. Pure fat is also widely consumed in other parts of Central and Eastern Europe.

HOW IT WORKS

These fats are not just used for cooking. They can sit royally on top of toasted or fried bread, be used as a starter for borscht, served as a main course or simply eaten with salt and honey. The fat sometimes includes a bit of pig skin, but no meat. A strange way to consume *salo* is by covering it in chocolate. Can I offer you a Ukrainian Snickers?

THE EXPERIENCE

Salo can be eaten cured or uncured. Without curing, *salo* is soft, chewy, creamy and greasy. When paired with a sour bread, the sweetness of *salo* is pronounced.

>> Get your chocolate-covered *salo* in Ukraine. ***Tsarskoye Selo*** *www.tsarske.kiev.ua; vul Sichnevoho Povstannya 42/1, Kyiv, Ukraine*

IN THAILAND THEY SAY THIS STREET SNACK WILL PUT A STING IN YOUR TAIL.

SCORPION: THAILAND

WHAT IT IS

Designed by nature not to be preyed upon, the scorpion has an exoskeleton like armour, and, if that isn't enough to keep it from becoming someone's meal, the arachnid's tail segment with its venomous stinger is the ultimate defence. Some scorpion stings can cause convulsions, muscle twitching and frothing at the mouth. Still hungry?

WHERE IT IS

Scorpions are found in most parts of the world; there are roughly 2000 species. However, the countries that view scorpions as a good source of protein rather than a deadly pest are largely found in Asia. On the Wangfujing Snack St in Beijing, black scorpions are sold on skewers. In Thailand, scorpions are fried or soaked in whisky. The Thai version of this delicacy is claimed to work the same way for men as Viagra.

HOW IT WORKS

The scorpion first needs to be detoxified of all its venom. Usually this means simply removing the telson (its stinger). Next, the exoskeleton is weakened so it's easier to eat. Frying or baking the scorpion normally works well. Serve with a sweet chilli sauce or sprinkle with salt and pepper.

THE EXPERIENCE

Scorpions taste like popcorn, albeit an oddly shaped popcorn that used to be toxic. The exoskeleton is pleasingly crisp, and the insides are light and airy, as the organs are evaporated by the cooking.

» Swallow the Singapore-style scorpions on shrimp toast at this restaurant in California. ***Typhoon*** *www.typhoon.biz; 3221 Donald Douglas Loop S, Santa Monica, California, USA*

BEST EATEN LONG, LOOSE AND FULL OF JUICE.

SEA CUCUMBER: CHINA

WHAT IT IS

First of all, a sea cucumber is not a vegetable, just as a sea horse isn't really a horse. A sea cucumber is an echinoderm and is related to the sea star (which isn't really a...never mind). Assuming you don't have issues with slimy textures and phallic shapes at dinner time, then sea cucumber is a pleasure to eat.

WHERE IT IS

This slippery, cylindrical, sausage-shaped sea creature is on the menu of virtually every Chinese seafood restaurant in the world. A dried version of the sea cucumber is available at Chinese markets and traditional Chinese medicine shops.

HOW IT WORKS

A sea cucumber shrinks dramatically when dried. It needs to be reconstituted by being soaked in water for about 12 hours. Once it has regained its original size, it's then braised for two hours. Finally, the sea cucumber is combined with actual vegetables like mustard greens and shiitake mushrooms, then served.

THE EXPERIENCE

Attempting to grasp a slick slice of sea cucumber with a pair of chopsticks is difficult, and eating this texturally challenging titbit might turn some off. By itself, sea cucumber is bland – the dish's salty and savoury flavours are derived from the sauce. If you hate slimy, then stay away from this phoney vegetable.

» Get some four-star sea cucumber into you.
Qi Restaurant *+86 10 6601-6666; Ritz-Carlton Hotel, 1 Jin Cheng Fang St East, Financial Street, Beijing, China*

每 一片
每 合 36
元

HORSES FOR COURSES – IN THIS CASE, THE SOUP COURSE.

SEA HORSE: ASIA

WHAT IT IS

These sea horses aren't the comic-book version, where the superhero Aquaman strode upon a magnificent sea steed as large as the land counterparts. No, these guys are tiny. They're bony, too. There's not much meat on them either. Why bother? Good question.

WHERE IT IS

If you want to find something strange and snacky, keep it simple and go straight to Wangfujing Snack St in Beijing. Here you can taste sea horse skewered and grilled to a satisfying crisp. Or try it in a medicinal soup to help rid your skin of acne.

HOW IT WORKS

To make sea-horse soup, bring a pot of water to the boil. Break up a few dried sea horses and throw them in the pot along with walnuts, pitted red dates, ginger and lean pork. Simmer for two hours.

THE EXPERIENCE

The flavour of sea horse is oceanic, a bit like salty scallops, but mellowed by the other ingredients. If simmered long enough, the small bones soften and are edible. The scant meat is far from satisfying, but this is more medicine than meal. If you get a pregnant sea horse, that's bonus meat. To make things stranger – in the sea-horse world, the males get pregnant.

» Forget the face peel, order a steaming bowl of sea-horse soup instead. ***Zing! Restaurant*** *+60 3 2117-4888; Grand Millennium Hotel, 160 Jalan Bukit Bintang, Kuala Lumpur, Malaysia*

STAR LIGHT, STAR BRIGHT, THE FIRST STAR I MUNCH TONIGHT...

SEA STAR: ASIA

WHAT IT IS

Without proper cooking the sea star, with its hard calcite-crystal plating, would be very difficult to consume. Fortunately, there are dedicated cooks out there who are determined to make the most challenging ingredients edible, if not palatable.

WHERE IT IS

A stretch of the Wangfujing Night Market in Beijing is nicknamed Snack St, where virtually any craving you have can be satisfied. The more exotic, the better. Deep-fried sea stars are sold on skewers alongside candied-fruit stalls and scorpion vendors.

HOW IT WORKS

The tough exterior of the sea star must be broken down. In Japan some people boil the sea star and eat the eggs inside. In China, medicinal soups have sea star as a key ingredient. Sea star fried in shark oil is how the vendors do it on Snack St.

THE EXPERIENCE

Crunchy and chewy when deep-fried, the sea star's underside is spread open to expose the gonads, which are eaten and have the flavour of bitter saltwater eel. The remainder is consumed afterwards like a snack from a deep-sea carnival.

>> If you can't get to Snack St, perhaps try here. **Hotel Hinoshimasou** +81 969 62-0568; 711 Hinoshima Ryugatake-machi, Kumamoto, Amakusa-gun, Kyushu, Japan

IF THE EARLY BIRD MISSES THE WORM, IT WAITS UNTIL THE FULL MOON FOR THESE LOVELIES.

SEA WORM: SAMOA

WHAT IT IS

The scene is surreal: clusters of people carrying hand lamps in the dark of night, wading into the ocean and pulling out strands of green sea worms (palolo) and eating them raw, directly from the water, like aquatic vermicelli. Then the diners thrust their hands back into the salty sea for another serving.

WHERE IT IS

Every year Samoans anticipate a wondrous natural phenomenon known as the Rising of the Palolo. It's really an annual spawning that happens seven days after the full moon in October and November. For Samoans it's a great excuse to have a festival and eat many sea worms.

HOW IT WORKS

When palolo worms spawn, they release foot-long segmented strands of themselves containing egg or sperm. Seasoned gatherers use torches because light attracts the palolo. Nets and buckets are used to capture large numbers of the worms.

THE EXPERIENCE

The taste is a peculiar combination of fishy, salty and tart, with an abrasive texture due to the worm's segmentation. Though locals prefer eating the palolo raw, calling it 'Pacific caviar', palolo worms can also be sautéed, roasted, boiled, fried, served at breakfast with scrambled eggs or baked into a loaf with coconut milk and onions.

>> The early bird gets the worm, but the early Samoan gets the palolo. *Tisa's Barefoot Bar* www.tisasbarefootbar.com; Pago Pago, American Samoa

POPULAR WITH BEACHCOMBERS, SUSHI AFICIONADOS AND MICHELIN-STARRED CHEFS, AND BETTER FOR YOU THAN JETSAM.

SEAWEED: JAPAN

WHAT IT IS

Seaweed is a highly abundant and nutritional food source, yet many people still regard it as being just short of trash – a weed. However, this common weed appears in Michelin-starred restaurants worldwide. If you've eaten sushi, you've eaten the seaweed commonly known as nori. If you've ever enjoyed a bowl of miso soup, you've consumed kelp. The fifth taste (after bitter, salty, sour and sweet) of *umami* was chemically recreated as monosodium glutamate (MSG), which is derived from kelp.

WHERE IT IS

Most accessible at shorelines, fresh seaweed is available around the world. It's extremely adaptable, and is also sold in dried form to be shipped anywhere. Seaweed can be placed into soups and reconstituted, or even eaten dry.

HOW IT WORKS

Go to the beach and collect the kelp that has washed up on shore. Clean off the sand and candy wrappers and make a soup with it. Or head to the local Asian market and buy a few sheets of dried nori and make your own sushi rolls. Snack on a few sheets while you're playing sushi chef.

THE EXPERIENCE

Seaweed is savoury, salty, oceanic and elemental, and its texture is as varied as the sea it comes from.

» You can order seaweed online. ***Mendocino Sea Vegetable Company*** *www.seaweed.net*

FROM THE DEPTHS OF WINTER AND THE BOWELS OF THE EARTH COMES THIS RANCID AQUATIC SNACK.

WHAT IT IS

Some say *hákarl*, from Iceland, is a taste to be acquired, while others feel this ammoniacal fish is simply a taste to be avoided. It seems that nobody, not even Icelanders, really enjoys eating *hákarl*. In this modern age of refrigeration, the delicacy's gastronomic raison d'être appears to be stout-hearted symbolism that acts as a reminder to Icelanders of their perdurable Viking stock. Or maybe it's just something to feed unsuspecting foreigners at a party.

WHERE IT IS

During the deepest depths of winter in January and February, a special festival called Þorrablót attempts to thaw the country's icy hold by celebrating Iceland's ancient culture with traditional food. The putrid shark can be found on a platter there.

HOW IT WORKS

A Greenland shark is gutted, beheaded and buried. It's then left in the ground to ferment for six to 10 weeks. Next, the shark is sliced into smaller portions and aired out in drying shacks for two to five months. Finally, the perfectly rancid meat is cut into bite-sized pieces, ready to serve.

THE EXPERIENCE

With *hákarl's* difficult smell and its taste of death and decay, endurance may be the key to ingesting it. If you can keep it in your mouth long enough to swallow, you may have a shot at keeping it down. Ironically, you can wash away the taste of death with an Icelandic drink known as 'black death' (Brennivín).

» Learn more about the Þorrablót Festival. ***Iceland Tourist Board*** *www.icelandtouristboard.com*

SHIMMY WITH A SHRIMP, A DRINKING PARTNER YOU CAN EAT.

DRUNKEN SHRIMP: CHINA

WHAT IT IS

Drunken shrimp can be interpreted as a cruel dish, since the shrimp are eaten alive. However, don't forget that in the wild they're also eaten alive, but without the pleasant embrace of alcohol to ease the pain. Ironically, drunken patrons are the ones who usually eat this dish of live shrimp doused in rice wine.

WHERE IT IS

This inebriated delicacy is almost always available at Chinese seafood restaurants that have an inventory of live shrimp swimming in the tanks. Your best bet is to bring someone who can speak Chinese so you don't end up getting the cooked version of the dish.

HOW IT WORKS

It's the simplest and quickest item on the menu. Grab a bowlful of live shrimp or prawns. Liberally douse the shrimp with high-quality rice wine, like you might with an old college flame. Watch the shrimp flop around. Try to grab one with chopsticks. Peel shell without getting splattered and eat.

THE EXPERIENCE

The twitching flesh is sweet and buttery. The texture is crunchy and chewy. The alcohol contributes to the shrimp's sweetness, and to your bliss.

» Well, at least the shrimp won't have that nasty hangover to nurse. ***Shanghai Ren Jia*** *+86 21 5403-7888; 90 Shaanxi Nan Lu, Luwan, Shanghai, China*

I'D LIKE TO TEACH THE WORLD TO STING, IN PERFECT COOKERY.

WHAT IT IS

The stingray is a fish that's related to the shark but is deadly in a different way. It attacks predators with a venomous barbed stinger at the end of its whip-like tail. It is just as delicious as it is menacing. The fins are where most of its meat is found.

WHERE IT IS

Icelanders like their stingray rotten and fermented. In Singapore and Malaysia they prefer stingray to be fresh, spicy or barbecued.

HOW IT WORKS

The stingray's fins are chopped into smaller portions for cooking. The sambal stingray dish is prepared with spicy sambal chilli paste, which is coated onto the ray. This is then shrouded with banana leaves and barbecued for about 10 minutes. Once cooked, a fragrant and spicy steam is released.

THE EXPERIENCE

Stingray meat is flaky yet dense and chewy. Its flavour is a coalescence of fish and lobster. The skin is reminiscent of thick-skinned catfish, slick and unctuous. The delicate taste harmonises with even the boldest of seasonings.

» Try this stingray with a spicy sting!
Leng Heng Seafood BBQ & Claypot Deluxe
+65 6445-0513, East Coast Lagoon Food Village, East Coast Park Service Rd, Singapore

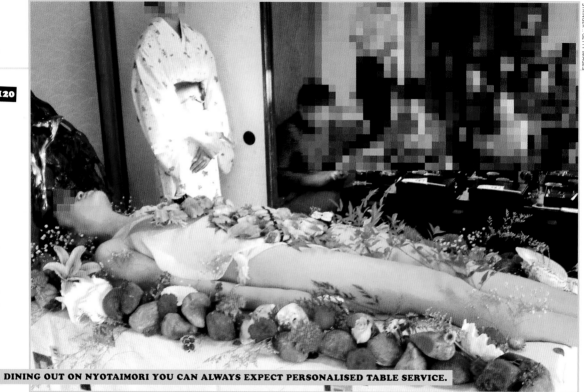

DINING OUT ON NYOTAIMORI YOU CAN ALWAYS EXPECT PERSONALISED TABLE SERVICE.

BODY SUSHI: JAPAN

WHAT IT IS

The food itself isn't the weird thing about *nyotaimori*. It's the presentation of the food. *Nyotaimori* means 'female body presentation'. That's when sushi is arranged on the nude or semi-nude body of a woman lying supine, allowing diners to eat off her.

WHERE IT IS

Nyotaimori used to be a nefarious, even dangerous, buffet in which to indulge. You had to have connections to Japanese organised crime or visit a Yakuza-operated mountain resort to find this salacious meal on the menu. Now, some restaurants serve body sushi as a gimmick to attract (or offend) customers.

HOW IT WORKS

If you want to be the *nyotaimori* model, there are some factors to consider. You need to be able to lie still for several hours without requiring a bathroom visit; you need to be free of any body hair, including pubic hair; you must bathe beforehand with fragrance-free soap; and you must avoid speaking to the diners. If you're eating the sushi, the rules are: no poking with chopsticks, no talking and no sexual harassment.

THE EXPERIENCE

Beauty and the feast. The sushi is the same as standard sushi, albeit slightly warmer because it sits on a hot-blooded woman.

» Like most food trends, this erotic service seems to come and go, but there are places you can go if really want to experience *nyotaimori* without going gangster. ***Kush Bar & Restaurant*** *www.kushbarsamui.com; 20/21 Moo 3, Chaweng, Ko Samui, Suratthani, Thailand*

OUT OF THE PANCREAS AND INTO THE FIRE.

WHAT IT IS

Many people still believe sweetbreads are exactly that – a sweet bread, some kind of sugared pastry. The anatomical truth is that sweetbreads are thymus or pancreas glands, thereby making the term 'sweetbreads' the most deceptive food euphemism of all time.

WHERE IT IS

The thymus and pancreas glands are consumed almost all over the world. Sweetbreads are generally a simple preparation of the organ by frying and crisping the exterior and sealing in moisture for tenderness. From London to New York, it's an international offal spotted on many fine-dining menus. Not bad for a nasty bit.

HOW IT WORKS

Sweetbreads must be cleaned well by soaking, rinsing and blanching before cooking. Then they're poached for about two minutes and cooled. Finally, they're fried until a pleasant crust is achieved.

THE EXPERIENCE

True, sweetbreads are far from being a dessert ,but when cooked well and dressed with parsley-root purée, blackberries and a squeeze of fresh lemon, this crispy and creamy chunk of organ sings notes as sweet as any *pan dulce*.

» Good ol' Tom Aikens offers not one, but two (lamb and veal) sweetbread dishes. Why not make the meal even sweeter and get both? **Tom Aikens** *www.tomaikens.co.uk; 43 Elystan St, London SW3 3NT, UK*

LITTLE MISS MUFFET GETS HER OWN BACK IN SKUON.

TARANTULA: CAMBODIA

WHAT IT IS

If you were forced into hiding to save your life from a bloodthirsty regime, you might develop a taste for spiders, too. During the Khmer Rouge's reign in Cambodia, mass starvation forced people into eating anything simply to stay alive – things like tarantulas.

WHERE IT IS

As soon as the Khmer Rouge reign ended, most villages gladly gave up entomophagy to resume the traditional Cambodian diet of vegetables, noodles and fish. But the inhabitants of Skuon, 75km north of Phnom Penh, continue the practice. This is where people from all over Cambodia head when they are craving furry, plump, venomous tarantulas.

HOW IT WORKS

Thousands of fuzzy black mounds in a basket undulate in unison like a possessed carpet. After the pile of tarantulas has been defanged (to remove venom), it is ready to be sold to vendors, who in turn will cook and sell the spiders to the hungry and the curious. Mostly these arachnids are deep-fried until crispy, or dumped into a vat of rice wine to create a tarantula tonic to remedy back pain.

THE EXPERIENCE

The civilised arachnid eater starts with an appetiser: the spider's crunchy legs. The next course is the cephalothorax (head and thorax), which contains delicate white meat with a hybrid flavour of fowl and fish. An optional course is the largest portion, the abdomen, which houses guts, shit and sometimes eggs – a wicked stew, for sure.

>> Go on to **Skuon**. Cambodia, that is.

IF YOUR CHEF IS PLAYING HARDBALL YOU MAY FIND THIS ON THE MENU.

TESTICLE: AFGHANISTAN

WHAT IT IS

Edible testicles come in various sizes and go by different names. Bull testicles are on the larger end of the scrotum scale, while rooster testicles (although relatively large compared to smaller birds) sit on the smaller side. When craving bull balls, the misleading American euphemism to use is 'Rocky Mountain oysters'. 'Rooster fries' is code for rooster balls.

WHERE IT IS

They're everywhere, these gourmet gonads. The Chinese enjoy rooster fries cooked in a hot pot. Afghans skewer sheep fries and grill them as kebabs. Bull testicles have inspired the World Championship Rocky Mountain Oyster Festival in Texas.

HOW IT WORKS

Slice the testicle, peel off the membrane, and season and cook however you like. The *Kama Sutra,* the ancient Indian sex guide, suggests 'Drinking milk, mixed with sugar, and having the testicle of a ram or a goat boiled in it, is also productive of vigour.' Improved 'vigour' is probably the main reason for eating another creature's jewels.

THE EXPERIENCE

Beyd ghanam is the Lebanese answer to lamb fries and is sautéed to a fragrant, moist perfection, thus elevating them to the status of a true delicacy. Seasoned with lemon and sumac, these spongy, soft bites of balls are sweet and zesty.

» Don't be frightened. Grow a pair and eat some balls! Or should that be the other way around...?
Alcazar *www.al-cazar.com; 17239 Ventura Blvd, Encino, California, USA*

NOT HELL IN A HANDBASKET, HELL IN A SOUP POT.

TOFU HELL: JAPAN

WHAT IT IS

Dojo tofu (also known as *dojo nabe*; eel soup) is as inventive as it is inhumane. It's a stew that involves live loaches (mudfish) inserted into tofu and cooked alive in a broth. It is also referred to as 'tofu hell', which is probably an accurate sentiment for the fish.

WHERE IT IS

This live loach tofu stew is a difficult dish to track down. The live version of this stew can easily be changed so as to not have the loach inside the tofu, thereby removing the delicacy's most controversial element. To avoid the tame version, make sure you confirm this before ordering.

HOW IT WORKS

Live loaches are placed into a broth as the heat gradually rises in the pot. At a certain point, when they become more agitated by the rising heat, a block of cold tofu is placed into the pot. The loaches instantly seek the relief of the cold tofu by wriggling their way into it. While inside the tofu, the fish eventually succumb to the boiling water. Now it's ready to serve.

THE EXPERIENCE

This stew is protein within protein. The tofu's vegetable protein encases the loach's animal protein like a soybean coffin. The fishy flavour of the loach is cut by the bland tofu. The fishbones are small enough to be eaten, which means no evidence of this hellish meal need remain.

>> What fresh hell is this? ***Komagata Dojo***
+81 3 3842-4001; 1-7-12 Komagata, Tokyo, Japan

BETTER THAN KILLING TWO BIRDS WITH ONE STONE IS EATING THREE BIRDS WITH NO BONES.

TURDUCKEN: USA

WHAT IT IS

This all-American holiday centrepiece is like a riddle wrapped in a mystery inside an enigma, but it's really a chicken stuffed inside a duck shoved into a turkey. Voila! Tur(key)-duck-(chick)en!

WHERE IT IS

The origin of the turducken is unclear, but two men are credited for its invention – an unknown farmer, and famed Cajun chef Paul Prudhomme. Created in Louisiana, the turducken is usually enjoyed in private American homes during Thanksgiving and Christmas.

HOW IT WORKS

You need to set two days aside for this massive meat endeavour. Get a chicken and a duck, both fresh and completely boned, and a partially boned turkey. Stuff them inside each other, then bake for approximately nine hours (depending on the size of poultry used).

THE EXPERIENCE

The mingling of chicken, duck and turkey meat, and their juices and essences, is said to be spirituous as well as spiritual. If you're a carnivore, turducken is the ultimate holiday feast. If you're vegan, then of course you hate turducken. Unless you make the vegan version – tofucken. Touché, vegans.

>> Turducken is a tur-mendous pain to make if you've never made one. But (if you live in the US) you can always order one. *Hebert's Specialty Meats* *www.hebertsmeats.com*

JUST LIKE A DEEP-SEA MINE, BUT TASTY.

LIVE URCHIN: CANADA

WHAT IT IS

The urchin's menacing, spiked-ball appearance belies the creamy, culinary decadence that rests underneath its protective plates of shell. It's the urchin's gonads that are the treasure. Once you breach the armour, there are five tranches of ambrosial sex organs lustfully waiting for you.

WHERE IT IS

According to Seafood Watch, a seafood-sustainability organisation, the best urchins come from Canada, where the echinoderm population is healthiest and most abundant. California is a good source as well. Urchin is common in good sushi restaurants, where it's known as *uni*.

HOW IT WORKS

It's best eaten very fresh and sometimes alive. But urchin is a hard (not to mention spiky) nut to crack, so be careful. You'll need to find the mouth side of the urchin and then, with scissors, cut around it until an opening is made. Gently clean out the other organs without disturbing the delicate golden gonads.

THE EXPERIENCE

The Italians work urchin into pastas and risottos. The Japanese like it on sushi. The adventurous eat urchins straight from the sea with nothing but ocean spray as a condiment. The taste is uniquely sweet and oceanic.

» Sample one and you'll discover the 'ooh' in *uni*. **Quality Seafood** *www.qualityseafood.net; 130 S International Boardwalk, Redondo Beach, California, USA*

OLIVER STREWE - LONELY PLANET IMAGES

GRITTY GOURMETS GRAB THESE GRUBS.

WHAT IT IS

It's nice to know that if you're ever stranded in one of the vast deserts of Australia there'll be snacks waiting for you, in the form of juicy witchetty grubs. For thousands of years this insect has been a vital staple food for indigenous Australians. Besides, it's either this grub or a crawl towards the shimmering mirage of a prawn barbecue.

WHERE IT IS

The chubby grub, which grows to be about 7cm long, can be found across central Australia in the root of the witchetty bush or gum tree, where it gorges on sap before metamorphosing into a moth – assuming that it hasn't been eaten by something or somebody first. If you'd rather avoid the harsh Aussie outback, it's possible, if you look hard enough, to pick up a can of witchetty-grub soup.

HOW IT WORKS

Locate a river red gum or a black acacia tree, look for clues of a grub population like a discarded larvae casing from which a moth developed, then start digging around the roots. A fat grub will usually be wiggling within a piece of root. Gently remove it without squeezing its fatness, however tempting. Either eat it alive or cook it under hot ash.

THE EXPERIENCE

The succulent witchetty grub will burst like a water balloon with the first bite. The juices from its insides spread around your mouth like a swig of red wine. The flavour is the essence of egg...or is it chicken?

» Hitch a ride to the middle of Australia, then tell the driver to leave and never come back. Search for bushes. Enjoy.

EXTREME CUISINE

October 2009
ISBN 978 1 74179 886 9

Published by Lonely Planet Publications Pty Ltd
ABN 36 005 607 983

Printed in China by Hang Tai Printing Company, Hong Kong.

© Lonely Planet 2009
© Photographers as indicated 2009
Cover Photograph: Radius Images © Photolibrary, iStockphoto
© Tomasz Zachariasz

Publisher Chris Rennie
Associate Publisher Ben Handicott
Commissioning Editor Ellie Cobb
Project Manager Kate Morgan
Designer Mark Adams
Cover Designer Yukiyoshi Kamimura
Managing Layout Designer Sally Darmody
Layout Designer Brett Perryman
Assisting Layout Designers Paul Iacono, Indra Kilfoyle,
Andy Lewis, Chris Ong, Cara Smith
Managing Editor Imogen Bannister
Editors Jessica Crouch, Penelope Goodes
Caption Writer Will Gourlay
Pre-Press Production Ryan Evans
Print Production Graham Imeson

LONELY PLANET OFFICES

Australia
Head Office
Locked Bag 1, Footscray, Victoria 3011
☎ 03 8379 8000, fax 03 8379 8111
talk2us@lonelyplanet.com.au

USA
150 Linden St, Oakland, CA 94607
☎ 510 250 6400, toll free 800 275 8555
fax 510 893 8572, info@lonelyplanet.com

UK
2nd floor, 186 City Rd,
London EC1V 2NT
☎ 020 7106 2100, fax 020 7106 2101
go@lonelyplanet.co.uk

Although the author and Lonely Planet have taken all reasonable care in preparing this book, we make no warranty about the accuracy or completeness of its content and, to the maximum extent permitted, disclaim all liability from its use.
